Londons Times Cartoons

Our Favorites

13th Anniversary Edition

By Rick London

Londons Times Cartoons
13th Anniversary

First Edition

www.LondonsTimes.us

Copyright © 2010 Rick London

ISBN: 978-0-615-41211-5

All Right Reserved

You can follow him on Twitter

@RickLondon

Book Design/Layout by Lee Hiller-London

Thank you so much for buying my 13th anniversary cartoon book. I hope you enjoy it twice as much as we enjoyed publishing it. That way, when we publish the next one, we won't feel so guilty charging a lot more for it.

Love to all. Rick London

Table of Contents

Forward 9
INTRODUCTION 11
Dedication and credits 17
    Dedication 17
    Credits: 17
This is the Gratuitous Title Page Just Before You See My Cartoons 21
    Lip Sink 23
    Madness and Genius 24
    Valley Girl 25
    Premature 26
    Picasso The Early Years 27
    Batchelor Party 28
    Recessive Jeans 29
    Salad Bar Exam 30
    Lost In The Crack 31
    Sinko de Mayo 32
    Sleeper Cell 33
    Slimy Terrorist 34
    Stairway To Heaven 35
    Sushi Bar 36
    Unicorn Self-Esteem 37
    Sperm 101 38
    Warhol The early Years 39

Conflict Of Interest	40
Dangerous Best Sellers	41
Banana Republic	42
Black-Eyed Peas	43
Planet Prophtlactia	44
P.E.T.A. And The Crabgrass	45
Moodie Moon	46
Disabled Cookies	47
Fly In Therapy	48
Food Chain Gang	49
Gator Community	50
Did The New Yorker Kill Humpty Dumpty	51
Earth Invasion For Dummies	52
Road Kill Petting Zoo	53
Kenny Loggins The Early Years	54
Cockroach Infidelity	55
Rorshach, Interior Decorator	56
Prehistoric Cartoonists	57
Skunk Grafitti	58
Signs, Everywhere Signs	59
Last Straw	60
Aardvark Dentistry	61
Dolphin-Safe Tuba	62
Wedgie Support Group	63
Woodchuck Physics	64
Poultry Nightmares	65

Elephant Courtroom Drama	66
Fly Swat Team	67
Hare Club For Men	68
Bad Cows	69
Picasso's Castro	70
Tolkien's Chef	71
Why Cartoonists Shouldn't Drink	72
Bedtime For Cows	73
P.I. Mink	74
Picasso's Peanuts	75
Pink Slip	76
Quarter Horses	77
Rabbit OBGYN	78
Mr. Ricehead	79
Hat Attack	80
Complaining Lobster	81
Ladybug And Chauvinist	82

Forward

I first met internet-wonder cartoon mogul Rick London, appropriately, on the internet, but more specifically, on Twitter. After several weeks of finding my way around that wild new world, a voice appeared in my Twitter Stream, a man with a strong, sparkling intelligence and a very good, finely warped sense of humor. I could depend on Rick to engage me with endlessly creative puns and inspire the same from me until the cows came in, and then I was sure he could concoct a cartoon about those cows that would be even funnier than the puns.

As a public philosopher, it's my job to examine life, analyze the human condition, and comment about it all in ways that will raise people's consciousness and perhaps provide new perspectives. Interestingly enough, that's exactly what Rick, as a creator of cartoons, doesn't except, he's funnier. If Socrates had just learned to draw, or partnered up with a really good, offbeat illustrator, he might have been able to create and sell some books himself. And maybe then things would have ended a little better for him. It's hard to poison someone who makes you laugh. One of the many hidden benefits of Rick's job is that he doesn't need a food taster or cupbearer to sniff out hemlock in his applesauce and white wine. The rest of us would rather slip in some vitamins to keep him going strong so he'll be around for a very long time to continue to build his online cartoon empire.

The existentialists were on to something. Absurdity sells. The majority of Reality TV shows and most ongoing developments in contemporary politics prove this repeatedly. But intentional absurdity and revealingly funny absurdity that's contrived to yield understanding is, of course, best of all. And that's what we get in so many of the cartoons that Rick, as a creative Socratic midwife, has birthed over the years. An off kilter remark, or a creative juxtaposition, can evoke both a smile and an insight
in one quick moment.

Two of the deepest secrets to extraordinary success in life are creativity and collaboration. Rick lives them both, and his work shows the results. He is also a man of great kindness and personal loyalty and qualities that shine as brightly as his intellect, and are as rare as his philosophically prominent funny bone.

I heartily commend these pages to you. Laugh, think, and enjoy!

Dr. Tom V. Morrris, PhD, Author of "If Aristotle Ran GM", "Twisdom" and
18 other books. Founder of The Morris Institute.

INTRODUCTION

I didn't start out to be a cartoonist; in fact, I didn't start out to be a lot of things. By the time I got to cartooning (age 44) I felt like life had passed me by and this was just something to bide my time. Never in a million years did I ever think it might be a business, and (what we Americans often call) "a commercial success" at that.

On March 19, 1997, I launched Londons Times Cartoons in an abandoned steel warehouse outside of my hometown of Hattiesburg, Ms. Nobody would rent to me in Hattiesburg because "I owned a dog". The truth is, they thought I was crazy. That's okay, it turned out to be a fantastic thing that they did. The owners of the warehouse installed electricity and a phone line. I owned a used IBM 386 clone, a book called "Internet For Dummies", and a stray dog named Thor who was my inspiration. My Mom had recently died and I'd lost my job in ad sales at a local CBS TV affiliate.

I began my research in January of 1997. I felt a great deal of relief when I started calling established cartoonists who would become my mentors such as Charles Schulz, Leigh Rubin, Jon McPherson, and Dave Coverly. Schulz told me he only became a cartoonist because "he couldn't do much else right". That hit close to home. The others seemed to reflect his sentiments. I found great irony in the fact that the world's most successful and established cartoonists were so generous with their time and knowledge, and those that were just a few years ahead of me, or even semi-known wouldn't give me the time of day. I like to think that, after our success, I helped others along the way. My theory is that the more cartoons that succeed, the more interest there will be in cartoonist, hence the more people will make a living from it, and more fans will turn to cartooning for entertainment.

I had a bigger challenge than "the basic cartoonist". My artistic skills were not very advanced. I could write gags "with the best of them" but when it came to expressing my gags into art, I missed the mark. This is where my mentors became invaluable. I learned that many cartoons we see in the newspapers and elsewhere are often team efforts with a writer/concept guy and an artist.

Though none knew of any where there was one concept guy/writer and a stable of illustrators, we'd all heard of Disney and I'd just read his biography. Though this type cartooning, to my knowledge had not been done with still cartooning, we had all seen it done via Disney's animation.

Please don't get me wrong, I do not compare myself to these giants. But they all helped me either through phone conversations, emails, or the books they wrote. I will always be grateful. I started with one local artist who rendered about 200 cartoons, mostly black and white, but I finally talked him into color. We made one big sale to a San Diego T-shirt company who paid us $10,000 for the rights to 20 images. We thought we'd arrived. Within a few months, my artist/partner's wife was pregnant and demanding he get a job in a bank and grow up. He did, I didn't.

Friends told me to abandon the project. I did the opposite. By now I had learned the Internet and recruited up to 12 illustrators and I was writing from 20-100 concepts per day. The whole project was on speculation. Artists came and went for various reasons. Then came one from Ohio named Rich Diesslin, he had been a published cartoonist for several years, also understood the Internet and how to turn it into a business. This was a blessing as right afterward; I had moved to Hot Springs, Arkansas and suffered a heart attack. I was unable to do much.

Right after that came 9/11. I was in bed but Rich helped me launch "Cartoonists Against Terrorism" which we still own, and in 2011 plan a store to benefit the families of fallen heroes. Our original idea was to have a book published but print-on-demand publishing was relatively unknown, and in New York, nobody would touch a picture book given the economy. Some of the top cartoonists worldwide donated cartoons to the effort.

I had been a very poor student growing up due to a myriad of learning disabilities. Later that year I returned to school at Western Governors University and finished 11 of my 20 assessments to graduate before more health issues evolved. I was forced to stop. I had planned to return but WGU said I had "finished my work too slowly" etc. and would not be able to unless I paid out-of-pocket the next semester. I had been going on scholarship, loans and grants. It was a no-go. I had too many expenses and put education on hold.

I looked up from my work and suddenly it was 2005. I was receiving emails from people worldwide. Major charities were contacting me wanting signed cartoons. Londons Times had about 3000+ cartoons up. I thought it was all a joke. How did all these people know who I was? One day in the middle of 2005 it was revealed to me. We were the number one Google-ranked offbeat cartoon. That had become my dream a few years into the project but of course I never expected it to happen. Our counter went from a few hundred a week to four thousand visitors per hour. We were actually luring over 1.8 million people per year and as I write this are nearing the 9 million mark (since 2005). It is still beyond my belief.

In 2006, I had the opportunity to begin opening online stores. I started with one manufacturing firm in Rhode Island. He seemed to know what he was doing, and my instincts were correct. Before I could blink, 3dRose.com had our images on 20 different products; and in associate stores all over Amazon.com. Our LTSuperstore.com saturated Google Shopping, Shop.com, Shopping.com, Bizrate.com and all the other shopping networks. We were suddenly a business.

I tried a few others known as POD's (Print-On-Demand) and we made everything from T-shirts to mouse pads to aprons to postage stamps and more at such firms like Zazzle.com and Printfection.com. We even opened the first green tee shop at Zazzle called RickLondonOrganicTees.com all made from 100% organic cotton and soy dye. Though it is a slower sales shop, it is one of my favs. Of all our businesses, I am most proud of it. If I could just make a living on it, I would close the rest. Cotton is a very dirty product (as far as pesticides) and I love it when someone purchases an organically grown cotton tee.

We were the first offbeat cartoon to be on US Postage. I don't mean the Stamp.com personal postage but stamps for resale. As of this writing we have over 200 images on stamps at our RickLondonCollection.com store. We were the first to put offbeat cartoons on Keds (or any shoes to my knowledge) and still do so at our RickLondonCollection.com shop.

I invented and created the first cartoon gourmet coffee gift baskets at our LTSuperstore.com and gave 3drose.com permission to use them for other creators and they work very well. We discovered mixing art and coffee is a good idea. Our baskets include a 16oz cartoon mug and matching coasters, not to mention whole bean coffees from five different countries.

I had stopped creating cartoons, I was on burnout. My best four-legged friend, "Thor" had just died at about age 21. I fell into a depression. I was not getting the enjoyment out of it that I once had. I found myself doing management and administration. It became a bit robotic. I began designing products and taking nature walks in our Hot Springs National Park to vent off steam and "heal my tired soul". I had always loved nature and grew up in a town where trees and such were not so important unless they were outside of town. Call me a "tree hugger" but my feeling is trees can be cut down if necessary; but I live right next to a National Park and I am a guest of trees, raccoons, deer, wolves, snakes, chipmunks, and many other lovely hosts and hostesses.

Then I met Lee, my love, my fiancée'. We will be married (as of this writing) in two weeks (June 18th). Lee grew up in Portland, Oregon, a place where nature and recycling and wildlife and important things, mattered.

There is a funny story behind our engagement. I did not propose to Lee, my sister, Kathy Ireland did. Yes that Kathy Ireland. Kathy is a wonderful sister and we talk just about anything. I told her I knew Lee was the one and she told me "I was taking too long". Too long to what? She said "To propose". Ohhhh. Lee had not yet met Kathy but Kathy addressed her at Twitter, "Would you be my SIL (Sister In Law)? We all had a great laugh (as did the millions on Twitter watching), but it was what I'd planned to do anyway so "Thank You, Sis". (She's an angel).

Lee was already eating healthy foods (I was sometimes); practicing Tai Chi, and at my suggestion, began walking in a nearby gorgeous park. Before I could say "Gone With The Wind" Lee was my better half and also a southerner. She fits in anywhere. And she fell in love with our mountains and park system. She hikes much further than I do; and has a beautiful blog and shop (products with her nature/wildlife photography) and digital designs. Her blog is HikeOurPlanet.com People order her gifts and collectibles worldwide.

Now we are working together on several projects. She takes a second (shorter) nature hike with me in the late afternoons (her long hike is in the morning). We both love the animals and nature and would rather be out mountain hiking than anything.

She has also talked me into starting Londons Times Cartoons back up for our 13th anniversary which we have done. I am recruiting a great team of illustrators and our cartoons reflect a new age that was not even here when I started Londons Times Cartoons; Google, Twitter, race profiling, wars, etc. It's fun again. Generation Two has begun.

I also launched a line of shoes that are the "world's only love quote shoes" called ShoesThatAmuse.com. It has been great fun to know that I know how to digitally design shoes on a computer and Lee has taught me how to do so even better and the new shoes are much more attractive. USA Today and AP Wire did a positive story on it.

So I look up again and I am 55 years old. I was born into a good family but molded to become a Realtor. It did not fit me well nor vice versa (it is a 3-generation commercial firm in Ms) and does very well. Still, not for me, though I did try for 3 years and even got my license after three tries.

Who would ever have thought that I am doing exactly what I want, being exactly where I am, and having the right soul-mate with which to do it. I say patience is the key. I waited a long time for this. Psychologists, friends, family etc. finally say "You deserve it". At the risk of sounding arrogant my answer is, "I know". :)

Dedication and credits

Dedication

This book is dedicated to my wife, Lee London, who has patience, kindness, humor and intelligence and most of all loves me, is supportive in my work and encourages me to be me.

Credits:

Bob and Barbara McDonald: Owners of the small warehouse where I lived and worked at the start.

Thor: The dog I found (or who found me) a few months before starting Londons Times

Dr. Ed Lundin: Professor at USM and Episcopal priest who saw talent that I didn't see and encouraged me to use it. He was very supportive when I lost my Mom.

My Mom (Dotty London) and her Mom (Ruth London - "Dear") Both of them had an uncanny sense of humor. They were determined that my life have every dimension. This was in the rural south when football and hunting/or fishing were enough to grow up to "be a man". They encouraged me to enjoy those, but to also explore the artistic and literary side of life; and approach it with a sense of humor.

The Illustrators: There have been many and I've enjoyed working with them all. I am enjoying the new 2nd Generation Of Londons Times Group as well. Special thanks to Rich Diesslin, manager of Londons Times for 11 years while creating his own cartoon. He is senior illustrator and has run the show on his own several times when I couldn't due to health issues.

To the city of Hot Springs whose residents have been supportive and kind, and welcomed me.

The City of Lumberton Ms. (especially the library) when my pc broke and they welcomed Thor and me for a year to work on the cartoons.

To our product manufacturers: 3DRose, Zazzle, Printfection, and Skreened

To Google & MSN: For keeping us ranked the #1 offbeat cartoon since 2005.

And to everyone I may have left out, you know who you are.

This is the Gratuitous Title Page Just Before You See My Cartoons

Lip Sink

Madness and Genius

Dr. Berkowitz discovers the fine line between madness and genius.

Valley Girl

Premature

Picasso The Early Years

Batchelor Party

Recessive Jeans

Salad Bar Exam

Lost In The Crack

Sinko de Mayo

Sleeper Cell

Slimy Terrorist

Stairway To Heaven

Sure it was pricey, but she was buying a stairway to heaven!

Sushi Bar

Unicorn Self-Esteem

Sperm 101

Warhol The early Years

Conflict Of Interest

Dangerous Best Sellers

Banana Republic

Black-Eyed Peas

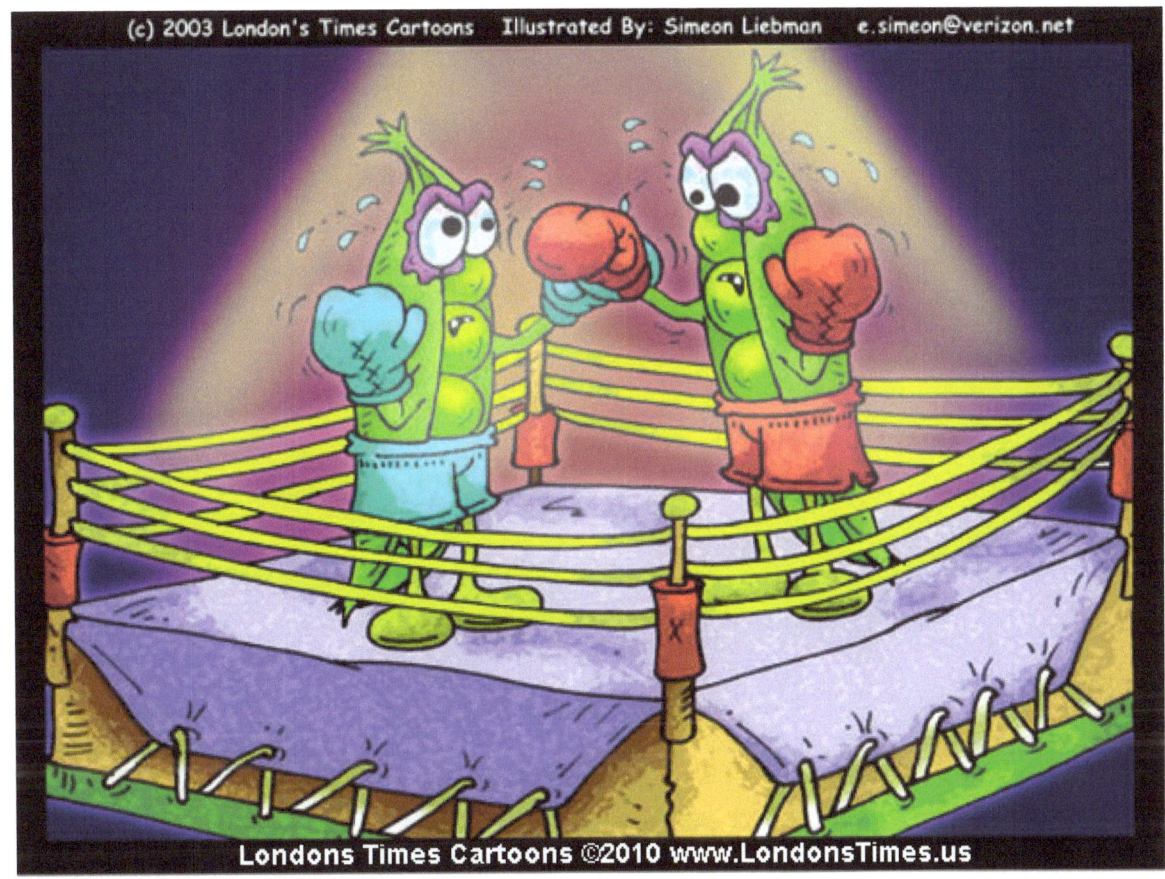

Planet Prophtlactia

P.E.T.A. And The Crabgrass

Moodie Moon

Disabled Cookies

Fly In Therapy

Food Chain Gang

Gator Community

SWAMPLAND, A GATOR COMMUNITY

Did The New Yorker Kill Humpty Dumpty

Earth Invasion For Dummies

Road Kill Petting Zoo

Kenny Loggins The Early Years

Cockroach Infidelity

Rorshach, Interior Decorator

Prehistoric Cartoonists

Skunk Grafitti

Skunk Grafitti.....

Signs, Everywhere Signs

Last Straw

Scarecrow and his wife find themselves in the divorce court

Aardvark Dentistry

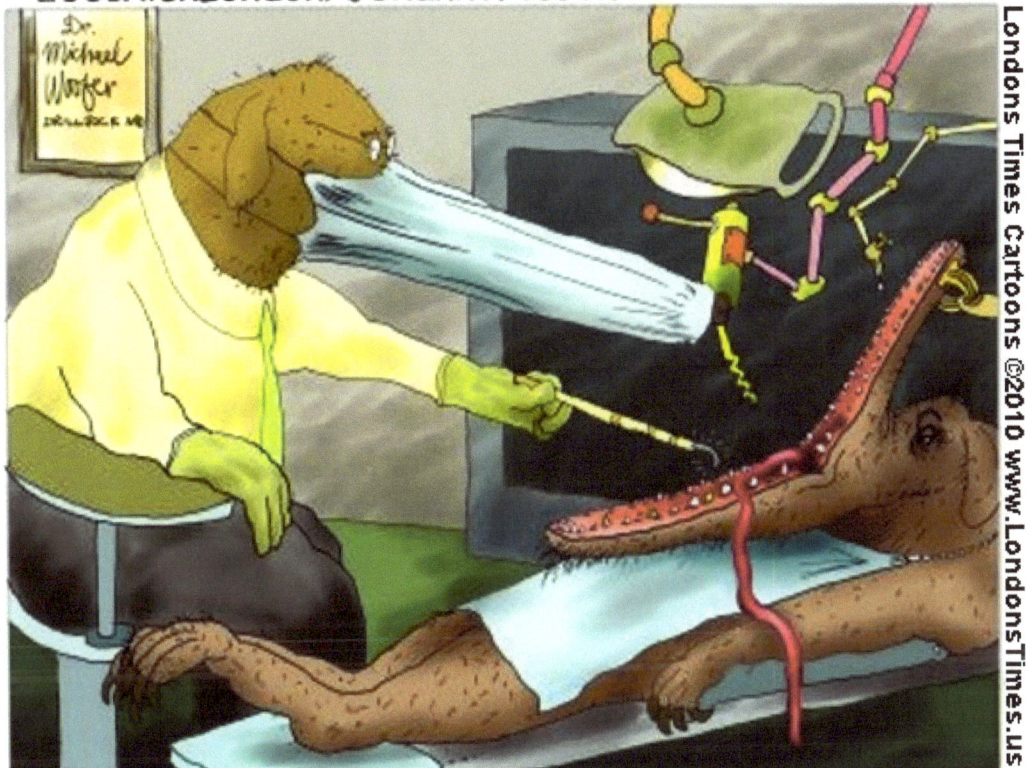

Dolphin-Safe Tuba

Wedgie Support Group

Woodchuck Physics

Poultry Nightmares

Elephant Courtroom Drama

Fly Swat Team

Fly swat team

Hare Club For Men

Bad Cows

Skinhides

outcasts of the bovine world

Picasso's Castro

Tolkien's Chef

Why Cartoonists Shouldn't Drink

Bedtime For Cows

P.I. Mink

Picasso's Peanuts

Pink Slip

Quarter Horses

Rabbit OBGYN

Mr. Ricehead

©2001 RickLondon/JohannWessels

even though his predecessor, Mr Potatohead was a success, Mr Ricehead hardly made it out of the box....

Hat Attack

Complaining Lobster

Ladybug And Chauvinist

A percentage of the sales from this book will be donated to various causes to help the people and wildlife of the Gulf Coast of America

More Books to Come...

www.ingramcontent.com/pod-product-compliance
Lightning Source LLC
Chambersburg PA
CBHW041545220426
43665CB00002B/41